Authentic Reading
Teacher's Book and Key

D1421935

Authentic Reading

Teacher's Book and Key

Also includes:
– 'warm up' activities
– active oral work
– vocabulary work
– guided writing tasks

Catherine Walter

Cambridge University Press
Cambridge
London   New York   New Rochelle
Melbourne   Sydney

Published by the Press Syndicate of the University of Cambridge
The Pitt Building, Trumpington Street, Cambridge CB2 1RP
32 East 57th Street, New York, NY 10022, USA
296 Beaconsfield Parade, Middle Park, Melbourne 3206, Australia

© Cambridge University Press 1982

First published 1982

Printed in Great Britain by
David Green (Printers) Ltd, Kettering, Northants

British Library Cataloguing in Publication Data
Walter, Catherine
Authentic reading.
Teacher's book and key
1. English language – Text-books for foreigners
2. Readers – 1950-
I. Title
428.4'076   PE1128
ISBN 0 521 28360 4

Library of Congress catalogue card number: 82–1179

MU

Contents

Part 3   Processes: How things happen   29

Part 4   Narrative: What happened   39

Part 5   Persuasion: Why you should do it   50

Part 6   Categories: How things are classified   61

Acknowledgements

I owe many of the ideas in this book to teachers I have worked with, trained or assessed over the years. I am sorry that my memory is not good enough to acknowledge them all by name.

I would like to thank Viviane Dunn for the *Car design* exercise in Unit 17; Alan Maley and Alan Duff (in *Drama Techniques in Language Learning*, Cambridge University Press, 1978) for the *Sketches* technique in Unit 23; Jacqueline Rodrigues for the *Discussion* technique in Units 1, 6 and 14; and Michael Swan (in *Spectrum Teacher's Book*, Cambridge University Press, 1980) for the *Misleading instructions* exercise in Unit 4.

Introduction

This book is intended for teachers using *Authentic Reading* in the classroom. Some parts of it will also be useful to students working independently at improving their reading skills. The main aims of the Teacher's Book, however, are
- to give teachers guidance in exploiting the texts and exercises of the Student's Book with their classes; and
- to provide additional activities for speaking, writing and vocabulary work based on the topics of the texts.

The reading process

Reading can be seen as a process of re-creating the text in the reader's mind. Another way of putting this is to say that the reader matches the elements of the text against her own world-structure, and modifies that structure accordingly. Research done at Brunel University* with the aid of a machine which records readers' progress through a text has brought powerful support to this idea. In a group of native English speakers, those who read most effectively, as measured by summary writing and by objective tests (multiple-choice and others), were those who read in such a way as to define the structure of the text for themselves – like building a summary in their minds. In fact, significantly more students did well when they were told that they would have to write a summary of what they read. More of these students had good scores on objective tests and summary writing than students who expected only objective tests after reading.

Authentic Reading seeks to exploit these findings in helping the language learner to read English better. In improving students' reading skills in a foreign language, we are faced with a complex problem. Many people are not used to reading in their own language the sort of texts which require them to work for understanding. So they have forgotten the skills that might help them to do this in English. Indeed, many of them might never have had these skills, as the Brunel evidence suggests. So we teachers must help them to improve, not only their English, but their reading skills generally. *Authentic Reading* integrates these two elements in a large variety of exercise types exploiting a series of authentic texts.

* L. Thomas and S. Augstein: 'An experimental approach to the study of reading as a learning skill.' *Research in Education* 8, November 1972, pp. 28–45.

1

One could object that using authentic texts does not necessarily make for authentic reading, since the students are reading for completely different purposes than they would in the 'real world'. This is true of any collection of language teaching texts; but I have tried to lessen the artificiality by

a) providing a suggestion for a 'warm-up' activity for each unit in the Teacher's Book. This is designed to get the students thinking about the topic of the text.

b) giving an introduction to each text, to situate it in context. Thus the student is not placed in the position of using the first reading to guess what sort of text it is.

c) replacing the *Summary skills* exercise, in some cases, by an exercise called *Reading for specific information*. This comes before the text and directs the students' attention to certain aspects of it.

d) letting the students choose, in some instances, which aspect of a text they want to concentrate on. For an example, see the *Summary skills* exercise of 'Save the children' on page 79 of the Student's Book.

Using the Student's Book in the classroom

The order of the units in the Student's Book is determined by the functional categories into which the texts fall. Thus, each group of four units contains texts with the same 'function' or purpose (e.g. categorization, instructions). In general, the more difficult texts are nearer the end of the book, and there is more explanation of the rationale behind the exercises in Part 1. But this is not a course in which the units must be done in order. Teachers who have organized their programmes around a series of themes can use the texts in the order in which they relate to those themes. Complete instructions are given for each exercise, even if one of the same type has appeared in a previous unit. If you do deal with the texts out of order, however, it would be a good idea to look through the instructions in Part 1 beforehand. These give students help in understanding the tasks they are asked to perform.

A note on the variety of texts in the book: It is certain that some texts will appeal to you more than others. But it might be worth considering that texts which you find less interesting may appeal to some or all of your students.

The time needed for basic work (reading and Student's Book exercises) will vary slightly from one unit to the next. This is because of the varying length and difficulty of the texts; and more importantly because a particular passage lends itself most suitably to certain exercises. It is a good idea to have a look at the unit you plan to use before going into the classroom: you are the best judge of your students' abilities. However, 40 minutes is the average time a typical unit will take. If you wish to spend less time than this, you might consider doing the *Summary skills* exercise in class and giving some or all of the other exercises for homework.

Warm-up, or getting students thinking about the topic of the text they are about to read, is an important part of the reading comprehension lesson. In the classroom we are trying to prepare students for the reading they will do outside it; and in their normal lives they will not usually be approaching a text 'cold', without any notion of what it is about. The Student's Book contains a short introduction to most texts, which places the text in its context; but in addition the Teacher's Book provides suggestions for brief sensitization exercises to use before the students open their books.

Summary skills exercises are an important feature of *Authentic Reading.* The reasons for their prominence are explained above. I have taken into account the different ways people have of organizing their perceptions in designing these exercises, and different modes of thinking are called for from one unit to the next.

In order for your students to get the full benefit of the *Summary skills* exercises, they should feel free to look back at the texts as they do them. This exercise is printed facing the text in most units, and I have made frequent suggestions that students refer back to the text. But you will probably have to remind them often that they can do so; it will ultimately be your attitude as a teacher which determines the students' success or failure in this area.

The other exercises which follow the text are not exactly the same in every unit. Each set of exercises helps students deal with the particular difficulties of the text it follows, and trains them to cope with similarly constructed texts in the future. You will also find that some types of exercise recur more frequently than others. This is because the skills involved are needed more frequently, or are more difficult to assimilate. Here is a list of the exercise types and titles you will find in the Student's Book:

1 *Summary skills.* Also called *Have you got the main ideas?*, *How good is your picture?*
2 *Reading for specific information.*
3 *Inference:* to help students learn to make inferences properly and to avoid making false inferences. Also called *How will it continue?*, *Opinions and feelings, Attitudes and feelings, General to particular.* Some of the questions in the *Accurate comprehension* exercises also train students in inference skills.
4 *Making connections:* this includes making logical connections between the different parts of a text and recognizing such things as the antecedents of pronouns (sometimes referred to as anaphora). Also called *Families of words, What does* it *mean, Why?, Find the reasons...find the ways.*

5 Overcoming difficulties linked to reading complicated sentences, reading
   details carelessly, missing negative expressions. Called *Accurate
   comprehension, Facts and figures, Dividing sentences, Why?, Negative
   expressions.*

The Teacher's Book gives notes on dealing with the individual exercises, as
well as a key to the answers. You should be encouraged, rather than
dismayed, if most of your students get most of the answers right: this is an
indication that the book is at the correct level for your class. The important
thing in improving students' reading skills is the work involved in doing
each exercise; the actual answers to the questions are merely a by-product
of this work.

Working in groups or pairs is one implication of this attitude to the
exercises. It is sometimes easier for students to accept and adopt a way of
approaching a problem if the suggestion comes from another student,
rather than from the teacher. Group work also gives each student more
time to be actively involved in classroom interaction and allows the teacher
to help with individual problems without stopping the entire class. Of
course, you will not be able to hear everything that is said, or correct every
mistake as soon as it is made. But you will be able to hear and correct as
much as you would in a traditional class, and you will gain the extra
advantages mentioned above.

A few of the exercises in the Student's Book specifically suggest working
in groups; most of the others are very well suited to this way of learning.
Three ways to organize group work are:

1 Groups of three to five people do the exercise together. Each group can
   then report to the class if you have the time and judge that this is useful.
2 Each person does the exercise individually. Small groups are formed,
   answers are compared and a consensus is reached in each group. Each
   group can then report to the class if you wish.
3 Begin in the same way as 1 or 2, but after the small-group work one
   person leaves each group to report to one of the other groups. This is
   suitable for exercises where you expect a certain variety of answers.

Additional activities

Authentic Reading is primarily designed to improve reading comprehension
skills; there is no provision in the Student's Book for vocabulary acquisition,
for instance, or for writing practice. But if you wish to use the theme of the
reading comprehension lesson as the basis for other classroom activities, the
notes in this book will give you detailed guidance on how to do so. For each
unit you will find suggestions for:

− *Oral fluency practice.* This is an activity in which the students approach the topic of the reading passage from an entirely different viewpoint. Besides giving them a specific framework in which to practise their speaking skills, this encourages the activation of passive vocabulary encountered in the text. There is a great deal of variation in the form of these activities: students are asked to organize discussions, carry out role play, conduct class surveys, engage in brainstorming sessions, agree with another student on a detailed plan, etc.

— *Vocabulary work.* This section calls on students to choose a few words from the text to learn. Learning will be much more effective if the students do choose the words themselves. It is necessary to use a dictionary for this activity; at this level the students should be using a good learner's dictionary in English rather than a translating dictionary. Try and make sure that they have, or have access to, the *Longman Dictionary of Contemporary English* or the *Oxford Advanced Learner's Dictionary of Current English.*

— *Guided writing.* This section provides opportunities for the students to use the patterns from the text in a short piece of personal writing. If you give some of these activities for homework, you may want to adopt the following system in order to give students an extra learning opportunity: instead of writing in the correct words when there is a mistake, write an abbreviation or a mark (e.g. *sp* for spelling mistakes, *v* for a mistake in the verb form) according to a code you have given the students. Then hand the homework back and let the students have a try at correcting their own mistakes. You can then do the final correction yourself; or you can add another stage where students work in pairs to help one another. You might even want to copy the different pieces of homework and distribute them to small groups so they can work together.

One further note: To avoid having to repeat 'his or her' each time the question of the sex of the student arises, I have chosen to use the general form 'her'. This is not to suggest that all students are female, but is used only for the sake of convenience.

I hope you will enjoy using this book, and would appreciate receiving any comments or suggestions you would like to send to me at Cambridge University Press, English Language Teaching, The Edinburgh Building, Shaftesbury Road, Cambridge CB2 2RU.

Catherine Walter

Part 1   Instructions: How to do things

Unit 1   Danger from fire

Before the students read the text, you may want to give them a short 'warm-up period (2–3 minutes), asking them to tell you all the things they can think of that cause fires in the home. Then make sure they understand that they are to read the text slowly and at least twice.

Summary skills 1

As with most of the exercises, it is useful to let the students compare answers with one another in small groups, once they have done the exercise individually. Answers:
a) 4 (there are furnishings – bedclothes – near a lighted fire)
b) 1 (there is an ashtray on the bedside table)
c) 6 (the table lamp is dimmed by covering it with a handkerchief)
d) 2 (there are three plugs in one socket)
e) 7 (is the nightdress flame-resistant?)
f) 3 (an electric blanket)
g) 5 (an aerosol container – is it away from heat?)

Summary skills 2

The completed table is on the facing page (answers can be in different words).

Guessing unknown words

Do not expect the students to explain how they arrived at the correct answers to the last three questions: different people may have different valid ways of arriving at the answers, and they may not always be able to express how they did it. However, if one answer gives particular trouble, you may want to show how it can be deduced. Answers (in these or different words):
1 plug   2 make weaker   3 old   4 easier   5 straight
6 have no choice / can't do anything else.

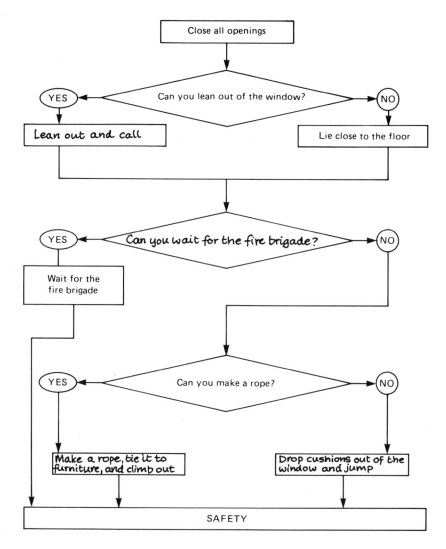

Accurate comprehension

Exercises like this one are designed to help students avoid reading things into the text that are not there. Answers:

1   False. It causes 1,000 fires a year, and many of them are fatal.
2   False. Going to sleep with a high-voltage underblanket on is dangerous.
3   True.

4   False. Buy a low-wattage bulb instead of covering a lamp.
5   Doesn't say. Untreated pyjamas and nightdresses are a danger for these categories of people, but the text does not say if the resulting accidents are often fatal.
6   True.
7   False. In some instances it might be better to lie close to the floor until you hear the fire brigade.
8   False. Use the sheets as a rope to climb out.
9   True.

ADDITIONAL ACTIVITIES

Guided writing

1   Students can do this alone or in groups of two or three. Give the students a list of other parts of the house: hall, kitchen, living room, children's rooms, garage and workshop. Let them choose one part of the house and make a list of instructions like the one entitled *In the bedroom*. Groups or individuals who finish early can compare their lists with others who are working on the same topic.
2   This could be used as a homework exercise: Write out a plan of action for your family (or the people you live with, or yourself if you live alone) in case of fire. Try to include all the possibilities, e.g. being cut off from safety. Be specific, and number the points in your plan according to what should be done first, second, etc.

Vocabulary work

An individual exercise, which could perhaps be given for homework: Choose four or five words or expressions from the text – words or expressions that you do not ordinarily use when you speak or write English. Look them up in an English dictionary. Write two sentences using each word.

Discussion

Divide the class into groups of four or five (a group can have only three people in it, but this is not so satisfactory). In this exercise, five points will be discussed. Each student will have the responsibility for one or more points. She must make sure that all the other members of the group express themselves on that point, and make brief notes on the opinions expressed.

Distribute the points for discussion, either by giving each group an envelope you have prepared, with the five points written on separate slips of paper; or by assigning numbers 1 to 5 to the students and then writing the numbered points on the board. Students will probably work better if you give them a realistic time limit for this exercise. Here are the points:

1 Give at least one practical suggestion on how the general public could be made more conscious of fire safety.
2 In Britain, if a child is badly burnt by an unguarded fire or heater, the parents or babysitter can be taken to court and fined. Is this fair? Is it useful?
3 It has been proposed that people should be held financially responsible for fire damage caused by negligence (e.g. smoking in bed). What do you think?
4 In Britain, there is no separate telephone number for the fire brigade. You dial 999 for the police, an ambulance, the coast guard, or the fire brigade. Is this good or bad? Why?
5 Suppose you could be on duty with a fire brigade for one month a year. Do you think you would enjoy it? Why?

You can always let the students run over the time limit for this exercise if all the discussions are going well; but setting a limit does seem to keep the discussions moving. As the groups discuss, walk around the classroom to give help to students who ask for it. It is best not to do any correction of students' English at this point; you may want to note down for yourself any mistakes that come up often, to deal with them in another class. The important thing is that the students communicate with one another in English.
    If a group finishes early, they can listen to a neighbouring group.

Unit 2   Wear and care of soft contact lenses

Before the students read the text, you may want to make sure they know what contact lenses are; and you might ask, for example, how many students would rather wear contact lenses than glasses if they had to make the choice. Tell the students that there will be words in the text they might not understand, but they should not worry about this as long as they can understand the overall meaning of each paragraph. Suggest that the *Summary skills* exercise may help understanding of the text; students should not hesitate to do it as they read.

Summary skills

A The first picture shows the correct lens shape (continuous curve, markings on the outside).
B From left to right, the numbers are: 2, 3, 1, 4.
C The number above the first picture is 1; the numbers below the pictures are, from left to right: 3, 2, 4.

Guessing unknown words

This exercise will give students help with the kinds of thought processes they can use to deduce the meanings of unknown words. A useful way to approach this exercise is to have the students do it individually, and then compare answers in small groups before discussing the answers with the whole class. Answers:
1 *small threads from the cloth, small bits of fibre*, or an equivalent phrase.
2 *concave;*

3 *stop holding*, or *let go of*, or an equivalent phrase.
4 *providing* means *if*.
At this point you may want to ask the students if there were any other words that bothered them, and have the class try to guess the meanings.

Dividing sentences

You may want students to work on this exercise in groups of two or three; or you may wish to use it as a diagnostic exercise, having students do it individually to see if dividing sentences is an area where they have problems. You can always make more exercises of the same type for students who encounter difficulty here. Several sets of exercises, with careful explanations when the student makes a mistake, should help in this area of understanding. Answers:
1 *...thoroughly/*
2 */dry...*
3 */and preferably...*
4 *...slightly/*
5 */as the marking...*

Inference

This is the most difficult of the exercises in Unit 2; it is best done in groups so the students can pool resources. Answers:
1 (line 10) No paper should remain on the skin when you handle contact lenses.
2 (line 16) Oily lotions should not be used before handling lenses.
    (line 17) Make-up, which often contains oil and is often put on with the fingers, should not be put on before handling lenses.
    (lines 6 and 35) Hands should be washed and rinsed before handling lenses, to remove dirt but probably also to remove excess oil from the skin and to rinse away any oiliness caused by the soap.
3 (line 17) There are instructions about when to apply make-up.
4 (lines 38, 42, 58) The instructions speak of the 'dominant' hand rather than the right or left hand.

ADDITIONAL ACTIVITIES

Oral instructions

Divide the students into pairs (one group of three is all right). Each person thinks of an action for her partner to mime; e.g. typing, climbing a mountain, driving a car. Then one partner instructs the other how to stand / sit, move, gesture, etc., without saying what the action is. The actor must guess the action, and then has her turn at giving instructions.

Role play

This exercise takes a little preparation. You will have to copy the six role descriptions, below, so there are enough for all the students. The students will work in pairs; but if there is an uneven number of students, you can add an extra parent (Role 1B) to the first role play.

Give each student one role; tell the students not to read one another's descriptions. (In most cases it is probably preferable to give Roles 2A and 2B to a male–female pair.) While the students are reading their role descriptions, you can answer any questions they have about meaning. Remind them before they begin their conversations that some of them will be standing, some sitting, and some looking for something on the floor. You will probably want to walk around the classroom while they are doing the exercise, to give help to those who need it; but it is not a good idea to correct students' English mistakes at this point. Perhaps one or more pairs will want to perform their conversation for the class.

Role play 1

1A You are 15 and wear glasses. The glasses make you feel unattractive, and you are sure you would be more popular if you had contact lenses. You work a few hours a week and have some money saved up, but not enough to buy contact lenses. Tell your father / mother that you'd like contact lenses and try to get them to pay part of the cost. Walk up to your parent and begin the conversation by saying, 'Dad / Mum, I'd like to talk to you...'

1B Your 15-year-old son / daughter complains of feeling unattractive. You are worried, and would like to help, but do not know how. He / she is actually an attractive person, but a bit clumsy, having broken three pairs of glasses in the past six months. You are hoping this will not happen again; you are paying for a new car and do not have much spare money. Sit down; your child will begin the conversation.

Role play 2

2A Your boyfriend / girlfriend wears glasses. You know he / she would like to have contact lenses, but can't really afford to buy them. You would like to buy the lenses for a birthday present. However, you know that your boyfriend / girlfriend is sensitive about having less money than you. Offer to give the lenses as a present, and try to make him / her feel comfortable about accepting them. You are having dinner in a restaurant. Begin the conversation by saying, 'Sweetheart, I know you'd like to have contact lenses. ...'

2B You wear glasses and you hate them. You would love to have a pair of contact lenses, but you just can't afford them. Your boyfriend / girl-friend makes more money than you, and you have thought about asking him / her to lend you the money for the lenses. You could pay him / her back over several months. But you already feel slightly uncomfortable about the financial inequality in your relationship, and are worried about feeling more uncomfortable if you borrow money. You are having a meal in a re-staurant; your boyfriend / girlfriend will begin the conversation.

Role play 3

3A You have just bumped into a stranger at a party and made him / her drop a contact lens. You are both looking for it but cannot seem to find it. If you cannot find the lens you will feel obliged to offer to pay for a replacement. Continue looking, and begin a conversation by saying, 'I really am terribly sorry...'

3B   A stranger has just bumped into you at a party, as you were putting
your contact lens in. You have dropped the lens and now you and the
stranger are looking for it. You have an important appointment tomorrow
and want to look your best; if you do not find the lens, you will have to
wear your glasses, which you hate. The stranger will begin the conversation.

Vocabulary work

Ask the students to choose four or five words from the text that they think
will be useful in writing instructions. Have them explain the reasons for
their choice to another student. Then ask them to write two sentences using
each word.

Guided writing

Ask the students to write one of the following sets of instructions. They
should try to be as clear and comprehensive as they can. They can draw
diagrams if they like.
1   Write out a recipe for someone who has never seen you prepare the dish.
2   Imagine you are going to lend your car to someone. Write out precise
    instructions on how to start the car and use the various accessories
    (lights, windscreen wipers, etc.).
3   Write out instructions for foreign tourists in your country, telling them
    what steps to follow if their money and papers are stolen.
4   Write out instructions for foreign tourists in your country, telling them
    exactly how to use a public telephone to call a number in Britain.
    Include details of what to do if there is some problem with the call.

Unit 3   How to shine at a job interview

As a 'warm-up', you might ask the students to vote by a show of hands on
following question:
What is the most important factor in getting a job: qualifications, an
impressive curriculum vitae, or the job interview?
   Many of the words and phrases in this text may be unknown to your
students. You might wish to explain that one of the aims of the book is to
help students get information from texts without having to know every
single word. Ask the students to read the text as slowly as they wish and as
many times as they wish, but not to worry too much about words they do
not know.

Have you got the main ideas?

Doing this exercise will probably involve reading most of the text again. Having the students compare answers with one another before discussing them with the entire class will not solve all the problems, but it will help the students see where the problems are.

Answers: The important points are numbers 2, 4, 5 and 6.

Guessing unknown words

You can use the correction of this exercise as a learning activity by examining with the class any wrong answers, and helping them see why those answers are wrong.

Answers: 1j, 2e, 3i, 4k, 5l, 6a, 7h, 8d

How will it continue?

This is a good exercise to do in small groups, as it will provoke discussion. The sentences that might be in the continuation of the article are numbers 2, 4 and 5. (Not 1 because it contradicts what is said under Myth 4; not 3 because 'making a good impression' contradicts the advice under Myth 2; not 6 because of the constant advice to be yourself and be honest.)

ADDITIONAL ACTIVITIES

Selection board

This exercise takes some preparation. Find a number of job offers in the situations vacant columns of newspapers. English-language newspapers are best, of course, but if there are none available use advertisements in the students' native language. In this case you may have to supply some vocabulary. You should try to get a wide range of advertisements – some that students might really apply for and some you know will be 'dream' jobs for them. If you have a large number of students in the class, you may wish to have more than one copy of the same job vacancy.

Divide the students into groups of five or six and pass the ads around. Each student in the group is interviewed in turn after reading out the ad she has selected.

Vocabulary work

Ask each student to choose four or five words or phrases from the text to learn. Students should look the words up in a dictionary, and find out from the dictionary or elsewhere whether the word would be acceptable to use in a business letter. They should then write two appropriate sentences with each word, indicating in what context the sentences might be found.

Writing practice

1 Students who want or need practice in letter-writing could write a letter of application for one of the jobs in the *Selection board* exercise, or for another job that they choose themselves.
2 Assuming that an American would approach a job interview according to the advice in the article, students could write a letter of advice to an imaginary American friend. The letter would outline the changes the American should make in his or her interview technique in order to adapt to customs in the student's own country.

Unit 4   American telephones

The *Summary skills* exercise is replaced in this unit by another kind of exercise. Often when we read a text we are not aiming to get a detailed picture of the entire text, but only to extract one or more bits of information that are useful to us. *Reading for specific information* gives students practice in this sort of task.

As an introduction, you might ask the students a question like 'Is the telephone system part of the Post Office in the United States?', to elicit the fact that telephone companies are privately owned in the United States.

Reading for specific information

You may wish to have students compare answers with those around them before correcting the exercise with the class. Answers:
1 Phone a service representative in the local business office between 8.30 a.m. and 5.00 p.m., Monday through Friday. If you are not satisfied, ask to speak to the business office supervisor. (lines 50–8)
2 Dial '0' (Operator) from another phone and report the incident. (lines 23–7)
3 Dial the Operator ('0') and ask for Enterprise 9800 (in Metropolitan Houston, call 223–4567), before digging the hole for the swimming pool. (lines 95–102)

4 Call the Operator by dialling '0' so that you will not have to pay for the call. (lines 44–9)
5 Look in the Call Guide (Customer Guide) pages at the front of the directory to find the number of the Southwestern Bell Repair Service. Phone them and they will repair or replace the phone free. (lines 15–22)
6 Make a list of the things you want to talk about before you make the phone call, then watch the clock while you speak. (lines 85–9)
7 Just say, 'No, thank you,' and hang up. (lines 73–5)

Guessing unknown words

This a slightly more difficult exercise than some of the earlier *Guessing unknown words*. You may wish students to do it in groups. Answers:

1 warranty	5 obscene
2 go through	6 drop off
3 refund	7 topics
4 toll-free number	8 cable

Inference

Ask students to note the line numbers of the evidence they find. Answers:
1 It is cheaper to pick up your own phone than to have it delivered. (lines 28–30)
2 'In some states you may be charged for some calls to Directory Assistance' (line 35–7). This indicates that people expect Directory Assistance to be free; if the company is charging for it now it is probably to discourage excessive use.
3 Children at home alone are advised to pretend their parents are there. (line 67–70)
4 You can pick up telephones at PhoneCenter Stores, but you can only pick up telephones you've ordered at Phone Pick-up/Service Centers. (lines 28–30 and 78–82)

ADDITIONAL ACTIVITIES

Class survey

In this exercise, each student must do a survey of the rest of the class, walking around and asking everyone else a question. When the survey is finished, each student gives a report to the class. Here are 15 questions; if there are more than 15 people in your class, you can give the same

question to more than one person and tell them to compare their answers
before giving a joint report.

1   Do you find it easy or difficult to have personal conversations on the
    phone?
2   Can you let the phone ring without answering it?
3   Would you like to have a phone in your car?
4   If you could order all your groceries by phone, would you?
5   Would you feel comfortable having a phone that transmits your picture
    as well as your voice?
6   If you were far from your family, would you rather get a short phone
    call or a long letter?
7   When is it too late at night to telephone someone you don't know well?
8   What is the earliest in the morning you would telephone someone
    you don't know well?
9   Are you shocked when someone telephones you and says 'Who's
    that?' before identifying themselves?
10 How much time do you spend on an average phone call: under 5
    minutes / under 15 minutes / more?
11 About how many personal and business phone calls do you make a
    week?
12 Is there a notepad and pencil by your phone at home?
13 When you phone, how many times do you let the phone ring before
    hanging up?
14 How many times have you spoken on the phone in English?
15 Do you dislike people telephoning to try and sell you things? What
    do you / would you do in this case?

Vocabulary work

Have the students choose about five words or phrases from the text to
learn. They should look each word up in a dictionary, preferably not a
translating dictionary, and write at least one sentence using it.

Writing misleading instructions

The aim of this exercise is to give students practice in writing instructions,
while allowing them to use their imagination and sense of humour. The
task is the following: working in groups, the students are to write out
sets of instructions for tourists coming to the country where the class is.
These instructions should be completely false, and designed to get the
tourists into the maximum amount of trouble. For example:

TIPPING ON BUSES   Always give a small tip (a few pence) to the person who sells you your ticket on a bus. Put the money discreetly into one of the uniform pockets.

Ask the students to set their instructions out like the telephone text, with a small title for each instruction. You may have to ask the class as a whole for a few more examples, to make sure everyone has got the idea.

Part 2   Descriptions: What things are like

Unit 5   A city is dying

To introduce the theme of this article, you might ask the students to show by raising their hands which of them would rather live in the city and which would rather live in the country. Perhaps one or two students might give reasons for their choice.

Summary skills

The students will probably get more out of this exercise if they do it individually first, and then compare answers within small groups. You will probably need to move around the classroom while the students are working, to make sure they have understood the directions completely, and to give help where it is needed. Note that the students can put something in a space even if they are not sure, and add a question mark. This exercise will prompt a certain amount of discussion, and you will probably want to go over the answers with the class as a whole when the groups have finished their discussions. The completed table might look something like this:

Problem	Cause(s)	Proposed solution(s)
1 Overcrowding	– Athens' geography – Athens built without plan – Migration from provinces	– Moving of government offices – Heavy taxes to discourage in-migration – Public spending for Athens? – Projects for countryside – Demolish half Athens, build again
2 Poor public transport	– High rate of migration? – Athens built without plan	– Demolish half Athens, start again – Public spending? – Taxes to discourage in-migration

Problem	Cause(s)	Proposed solution(s)
3 Noise	– Drivers' shouting and honking car horns	– Public spending? – Demolish and start again?
4 Air pollution	– Cars (50% of air pollution)	– Oxygen-producing plants? – Public spending? – Moving of government offices – Discourage in-migration – Demolish, start again

Guessing unknown words

Answers (in these or other words):

1 not having
2 crowded, pushed together
3 left
4 have, face

5 a long time
6 move
7 begun

Facts and figures

Notice that the answers to these questions are not found directly in the text. The students must use the figures in the text and do simple calculations to arrive at the answers:

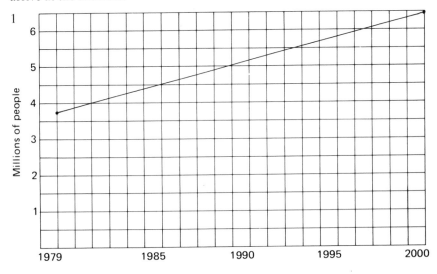

2 36,000
3 27,407
4 9,250,000
5 75 mg of sulfur dioxide per cubic meter

ADDITIONAL ACTIVITIES

Brainstorming

This activity is best done in small groups of about five people. Each group chooses one of the problems of Athens:
– noise
– air pollution
– overcrowding
– poor public transport

The group then has three tasks:
1 The brainstorming itself. During this time the members of the group must try to think of as many ways as possible to help solve their problem. One group member should act as secretary and write all the ideas down. Any idea, no matter how nonsensical it seems, should be expressed: it is quantity, not quality, that matters at this stage, and a seemingly ridiculous idea can sometimes spur a creative but practical one. You might want to give a time limit to this part of the exercise.
2 Feasibility rating. The group should give each idea a feasibility rating from 1 for an easy-to-carry-out, inexpensive project to 4 for a nigh-impossible idea.
3 Effectiveness rating. The group should take the ten or so most feasible ideas and rate them according to how far they will go towards solving the problem: A for a very effective idea, B for an effective idea, etc.
You may want the groups to report their findings to the class when they have finished, but this is really a case where the process is more important than the product, and the reporting can easily be dropped.

Vocabulary work

Students should each choose five words or so from the text to learn. They should look the words up in a dictionary, and also find out, from the dictionary or elsewhere (perhaps from you), whether their words could be used in a scientific report or whether they are too familiar or emotive for that use. They should write a sentence or two using each word.

Writing practice

Ask the students to describe their own or another city / town / village, using the article as a model.

Unit 6   Loneliness

You might introduce the theme of this unit by having the class discuss this question for a couple of minutes:
    What sort of people do you think are lonely?

How good is your picture of Mrs Calthorpe and her home?

You may want to give students a few minutes to answer these questions individually before discussing them in class.
Answers (in these or other words):
1 The street is full of broken glass and abandoned houses.
2 It was infested, so the Calthorpes probably did not want it in the house.
3 Mrs Calthorpe only earns about £10 a week; with her work and the children, she probably does not have much time to look after the house.
4 She is poor, she works and looks after her children, her husband is in prison, ...

Guessing unknown words

Do not insist on exact definitions of the words in this exercise; encourage students to tell you whatever they can deduce about the words. The answers should be something like:
1 full, or encumbered, or obstructed
2 breaking, or walking on
3 fallen down, or broken
4 dirty, spotted

Have you got the picture?

Instead of having all the students do all three of the questions, you may wish to divide the class into three groups and have each group work on one question. Suggest that they close their books to work on the question. They will probably be surprised at how much they remember. They can then open their books and check their information themselves.

Accurate comprehension

Answers: 1T, 2T, 3F, 4T, 5DS, 6F

ADDITIONAL ACTIVITIES

Discussion

Divide the class into groups of four or five (a group can have only three people in it, but this is not so satisfactory). In this exercise, five points will be discussed. Each student will have the responsibility for one or more points. She must make sure that all the other members of the group express themselves on that point, and make brief notes on the opinions expressed.

Distribute the points for discussion, either by giving each group an envelope you have prepared, with the five points written on separate slips of paper; or by assigning numbers 1 to 5 to the students and then writing the numbered points on the board. Students will probably work better if you give them a realistic time limit for this exercise. Here are the points:

1 Why do you think Mrs Calthorpe is lonely?
2 Why do you think Miss Quentin is lonely?
3 Do you feel more sympathetic towards Mrs Calthorpe or Miss Quentin? Why?
4 What has been the loneliest time of your life?
5 Would you / do you like to live alone? Why?

Vocabulary work

Ask each student to choose about four words from the text to learn. She should tell another student why these words were chosen. After looking up the words in a dictionary, the student should write a sentence or two with each word.

Guided writing

Each student should write a short description of a person in her environment (home or work). This can be a person she knows, a fictional character, or someone from a picture in a magazine.

Unit 7   Holidays in Scotland

Like Unit 4, this unit does not contain a *Summary skills* exercise; it has been replaced by another kind of exercise. Often when we read a text we are trying not to get a detailed picture of the entire text, but only to extract those bits of information that are useful to us. *Reading for specific information* gives students practice in this type of task.

Reading for specific information

Once students have done this exercise individually, they can usefully be put into small groups to compare answers before you discuss the answers with the entire class:
1   Aviemore (£140.00 each), Inverness (£143.50 each), Perth (£168.00 each), Pitlochry (£150.50 each)
2   North Berwick
3   North Berwick
4   Gatehouse of Fleet (£360.50), Pitlochry (£346.50)
5   Glenborrodale (£350.00), Perth (£336.00), North Berwick (£357.00)

Guessing unknown words

When you are correcting this exercise, find out what wrong answers were given and discuss why they are wrong. This will help students the next time they need to guess unknown words.
    Answers: 1k, 2h, 3m, 4c, 5l, 6g, 7i, 8e

ADDITIONAL ACTIVITIES

Planning a holiday

Each student should choose three hotels from the list – three hotels where she would enjoy spending a holiday. Then the students should walk around the classroom, each trying to find another student who has chosen at least one of the same hotels. The pair should decide on one hotel, discuss the reasons for their choice, and decide when they would like to go and how long they would like to stay.

Vocabulary work

Ask students to choose from the text four or five adjectives which are used to make the hotels sound attractive. They should look the words up in a dictionary. Then they should write a sentence or two using each one, or try to use them in the *Guided writing* exercise.

Guided writing

Ask students to write two short place descriptions like the ones in the advertisement. They can describe the place where they live, places where they have been, or places where they would like to go, trying to make them sound as appealing as possible.

Unit 8   Zen and the art of motorcycle maintenance

To introduce students to the theme of the text, you could begin by asking them to tell you as many ways of travelling as they can think of. Write the ways on the board as they tell you. Then go back over the list and ask students to vote by a show of hands for their favourite way of travelling.

Summary skills

Students can compare answers in small groups once they have done the exercise individually. Answers:

The narrator is travelling across an area of the ~~Rocky Mountains~~ *Central Plains* by motorcycle. It is a hot, ~~dry~~ *muggy* morning, and there are a lot of ~~hills~~ *marshes* along the ~~wide new~~ *narrow old* highway the narrator is using. The air from the marshes is ~~warm~~ *cool*.

This ~~is~~ *isn't* the first time the narrator has been in this country. He is ~~unhappy~~ *happy* to be back in this ~~irritating~~ *relaxing* place and see the plants and animals again. His son Chris, who is riding ~~beside~~ *behind* him on ~~another~~ *the same* cycle, ~~is~~ *isn't* impressed with the bird his dad notices.

Chris is 11; the narrator thinks that is too ~~old~~ *young* to be impressed with blackbirds. The blackbird is interesting to the narrator because it reminds him of ~~a story~~ *memories* he ~~read~~ *has*: ~~deer~~ *duck* hunting in the marshes in the autumn, walking ~~through~~ *across* the ~~mud~~ *ice and snow* in the winter.

Travelling on a motorcycle is ~~not so good as~~ *better than* travelling by car because on a motorcycle you are a participant rather than a spectator. You ~~can~~ *can't* ignore the experience of travelling. The narrator and his son have very ~~definite~~ *indefinite* plans about their vacation, because it is the ~~destination~~ *travelling* that interests them more than the ~~journey~~ *destination*.

Have you got the main ideas?

This exercise will give rise to a lot of discussion in the class, so it is probably most usefully done in small groups. You can walk around to give students any help they need. When the groups have finished you can discuss the answers with the class as a whole, getting students to tell you why the wrong answers are wrong.

Answers: the scenery, the narrator's past experience of this place, the pleasure and interest of travelling by motorcycle.

Guessing unknown words

This would be a good exercise to do in pairs or small groups. Answers :

1 marsh	7 helmet
2 two-laner	8 hollers
3 muggy	9 focus
4 cattails	10 whizzing
5 bump	11 overwhelming
6 muck	

ADDITIONAL ACTIVITIES

Holiday survey

In this exercise, each student interviews as many of the other class members as she can in 15 minutes. She then writes a very short report on the findings of the survey and presents it to the class. Here are 15 questions: if there are more than 15 people in your class, you can give the same question to more than one person and tell them to compare their answers before giving a joint report. (Omit any questions that are not appropriate to your class; for example No. 9 if you think that very few people in the class have been in an aeroplane.)

1   On holiday, do you prefer staying in one place or touring? Why?
2   Do you enjoy camping, or would you like to go camping? Why?
3   Do you / would you enjoy riding a motorcycle? Why?
4   Do you prefer travelling by motorway or by smaller roads? Why?
5   Have you ever taken a walking holiday? Would you like to do it (again)?
6   What sports do you enjoy on holiday? Do you play any sports all year round?
7   Have you ever been abroad on holiday? Where?
8   Would you rather go on holiday to an exciting foreign city or to some beautiful mountain / seaside place in your own country? Why?
9   Do you enjoy being in an aeroplane or not? Why?
10   Would you like to take a round-the-world cruise on an ocean liner? Why?
11   What country in the world would you most like to visit?
12   Have you ever hitchhiked? Would you like to do it (again)?
13   Do you / would you enjoy travelling alone? Why?
14   What is your chief aim in going on holiday?
15   Do you / would you enjoy going on a package holiday where everything is planned for you? Why?

Vocabulary work

Have the students choose four or five words to learn from the text. They should look the words up in the dictionary, and find out from the dictionary or elsewhere (perhaps from you) whether the words are only used in a familiar style. They should use the words in sentences, perhaps in the writing exercise that follows.

Writing practice

You might give the students a choice between these two tasks:
1 Reread lines 35–50. Then write a description of your memories of a place and the things you did there.
2 Reread lines 51–66. Then write a description of some sport or pastime you enjoy. The description should show someone not familiar with the activity why you enjoy it.

Part 3   Processes: How things happen

Unit 9   Drinking while driving—How does the test work?

You might introduce this text by telling the students the title and asking them to give you words they think might come up.

Summary skills 1

Make sure the students understand that they have only to write brief notes, not complete sentences, in the blanks in the diagram. This is a good exercise to do in small groups.

The completed table is on page 30 (answers can be in different words).

Summary skills 2

When you are correcting this exercise with your students, it will help those who have made mistakes if you ask which incorrect answers they chose. You can then help them to see why their answers were incorrect, which will help them develop their summary skills.

Answers: 1f, 2h, 3a, 4e, 5j, 6l, 7d, 8b, 9k

Guessing unknown words

You may wish students to compare answers with one another before correcting the exercise with the whole class. Answers (in these or other words):
1 breaking the law in a small way, making a driving mistake
2 something has to be done quickly, life is in danger
3 small amount
4 cutting, making a small hole in
5 kept
6 made to pay money as a punishment

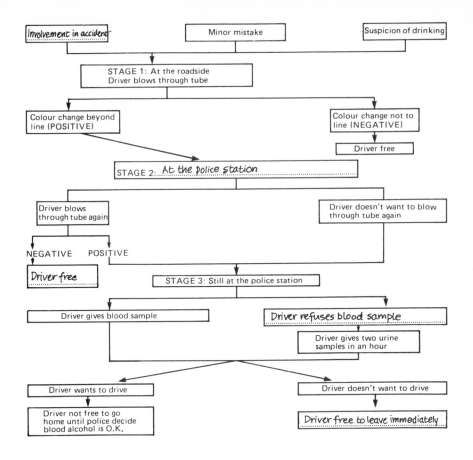

ADDITIONAL ACTIVITIES

Role play: Review committee

(This exercise takes some preparation on your part. You will need to make copies of the role descriptions so that each student has instructions about her role.)

Tell the students they are to imagine that they are a committee formed to review the law on drink and driving. Each of them will receive a role to play on the committee. They must discuss the law, and agree on a joint recommendation to make.

Divide the class into groups of five or so, and distribute the role descriptions. If there is a group of four, you can drop any role but the Judge; for a group of six, add a doctor, who will have the same brief as the Travelling Salesman.

It is probably best to give the students a time limit for this exercise, and not let things drag on too long. While they are discussing, make yourself available for help; but it is probably not a good idea to correct the students' English at this point.

Role descriptions

PEDESTRIAN'S REPRESENTATIVE You are the representative of a pedestrian's association. You have a very good friend who was paralysed in a car accident caused by a drunken driver. You do not want the laws relaxed in any way.

POLICE CHIEF You are a police chief. You would like to see the law extended so that the police can test any driver, not just those who have given some evidence of carelessness. You think people will be more careful if they know they can be stopped and tested at any time.

TRAVELLING SALESMAN/WOMAN You are the respresentative of the travelling salesmen and saleswomen's association. You would like to see the law on disqualification relaxed, so drivers who need their cars for their jobs do not suffer so much. You think the first conviction should only carry a fine for these people.

EURO-MP You are a Member of the Parliament of the European Economic Community (Common Market). The Community is trying to standardize driving regulations. None of the other countries has such strict punishment for the first conviction. Try to get the laws relaxed.

JUDGE You are a judge, the chairperson of the committee. Make sure that everyone voices his or her opinion, and try to negotiate a single committee recommendation.

Vocabulary work

Ask each student to choose four or five words to learn from the text. She should tell another student what the words are and why she has chosen them. After looking the words up in a dictionary, students should use them in sentences – either in the writing exercise which follows or as a separate activity.

Writing practice

Students should describe some process in their own country. They should choose a process they are familiar with so they can describe it in detail. Ask them to try to write connected prose, and to look back at the text if

they need help with this. Some of the processes they might write about
are:
– Getting into University.
– Getting a divorce.
– Getting medical care paid for, either by a national health scheme or a
  private insurance company.

Unit 10   Drinks from fruits and grains

As a 'warm-up', you might ask the students to name as many drinks as
they can think of that are made from fruits and grains.

Reading for specific information

Give the students a minute or so to look at the table without marking
anything on it or reading the text. Then tell them to fill in the table as
quickly as they can by finding the answers in the text. You may wish
them to compare answers with one another before checking with you.
Answers:

	Red wine	White wine	Beer	Port	Gin	Scotch whisky	Brandy
Made from dark grapes	X	X		X			X
Made from white grapes		X		X			X
Made from grain			X			X	
Must be drunk quickly	X	X	X				
Can be drunk long after it is opened				X	X	X	X
Contains no distilled alcohol	X	X	X				
Contains some distilled alcohol				X			
Made completely of distilled alcohol					X	X	X

Guessing unknown words

Answers (not necessarily in these words):
1 kind, sort
2 It crushes grapes.
3 berry, bush or vine
4 made
5 a plant

Inference

Once the students have done this exercise individually, they can check their answers by working in small groups. There will probably be no need for you to do a general check with the whole class; just circulate in the classroom to solve any problems that come up. Answers:
1 No; we only know that it was 'early in the development of agriculture' and that the ancient Egyptians drank it.
2 No (line 10: 'when there is no air present').
3 The skin of dark grapes (see lines 12 and 13).
4 No (see line 24).
5 Probably not (since line 30 specifies Scotch whisky).

ADDITIONAL ACTIVITIES

Information pooling

In this exercise, students will try to find out about a subject by asking the other members of the class. Each student should choose a subject from the list below. (You may wish to add to the list or subtract from it according to what you know about your students' tastes and knowledge.) Then the student moves around the room finding out if any other student can give information on the subject. If she cannot find anything out at all, she should choose a new subject.
1 Different types of red wine.
2 Different types of white wine.
3 The cost of different sorts of alcoholic drinks in this country.
4 Car engines running on alcohol.
5 Different types of whisky.
6 How to flambé a steak with cognac.
7 How to make a martini (or some other cocktail).

Vocabulary work

Students should choose three or four words to learn from the text, look them up in a dictionary, and write one or two sentences with each word.

Guided writing – How things are made

Ask students to choose something they know how to make themselves; or something they have seen made. They should describe the process of making the product, trying to be as precise as possible. They should also try to aim for a text that reads well, and not just a list of sentences.

Unit 11   The town that kids built

This is a longer text than some of the others in the book, and while it is not difficult to understand, it contains a great deal of detail. The *Summary skills* exercises will try to help students organize this detail in their minds. As an introduction to the subject, you might take a vote, asking how many students think that their elementary school was a good one and how many do not.

Summary skills 1

It is important that students realize the possibility of more than one 'correct' order in this exercise. This is a good exercise for group work after individual preparation. The most important points, in one logical order, are: g, e, c, b.

Summary skills 2

Once again, students will probably profit most from this exercise if they do it individually first and then form small groups to pool and evaluate their answers. Some of the details students might give for each point are:
1 – They are free in what they design because it is in a future context.
  – During the model-building phase the students' elected representatives make all the decisions.
2 – They build an imaginary landscape and construct shelters on it.
  – They simulate weather conditions and see the effect it has on their shelters.
  – Later, they organize into tribes for survival and division of labour.
3 – First they work with a model classroom to find the best arrangement; then they transfer that arrangement to the real classroom.
4 – The future city is divided into land parcels using natural boundaries.
  – Areas are marked off for different sorts of development.
  – The parcels are distributed to all the students.

Guessing unknown words

You can use the correction of this exercise as a learning activity by examining any wrong answers with the class, and helping them see why those answers are wrong.
　　Answers: 1e, 2c, 3h, 4a, 5b, 6d, 7g

Accurate comprehension

The 'doesn't say' feature of this exercise is designed to make students read more carefully and avoid making unwarranted inferences.
　　Answers: 1F, 2F, 3T, 4DS, 5F, 6T

ADDITIONAL ACTIVITIES

Redesigning the environment

This is an activity similar to the ones the children in CBEP participate in. The students are divided into small groups of three or four. Each group then goes through the following steps:
1　Make a list of the good things and the bad things in the way your school or classroom is designed.
2　Redesign the available space, keeping or improving the good things and trying to remedy the bad things. Draw a rough plan corresponding to your design.
3　Present the design to the rest of the class (the whole group may do this, or they may elect a spokesperson). Explain why you have made the changes and how the new design will work.
4　After all the new designs have been presented, vote on which is the best. Some groups may want to produce a humorous design rather than a serious one.
　　Walk around the classroom as the groups are working to give any help that is needed, but try not to give your opinion about the ongoing work or correct any of the mistakes in English. If you wish to note some of the commoner mistakes for yourself, students can then practise the correct forms in a later class.

Vocabulary work

Ask each student to choose four or five words to learn from the article. She should then tell another student why these words were chosen. After looking the words up in a good dictionary, the students should write a sentence or two using each word.

Writing practice

Ask students to describe how people are / were organized in a place where they have worked or lived. This could be their primary school classes, the place where they work now, the government of their country... .

Unit 12   Inside story

This is not a particularly complex text, but the ideas in it will probably be new to most students. Make sure your students have enough time to read the text thoroughly.

Have you got the main ideas?

Encourage students to look back at the text as they do this exercise. You may wish to have them note the numbers of the lines where they find the answers. Be sure you help them understand why any wrong answers are wrong.
   Answers: 1T, 2T, 3F, 4T, 5T, 6F

Families of words

This exercise is different from the *Guessing unknown words* exercises you have seen in other chapters. Your students will certainly know the italicized words in the questions. The aim of the exercise is not, therefore, to help them guess these words, but to show how meaning is structured in the passage by the use of words that repeat ideas already mentioned. Answers:
1 vaguer
2 weight, resistance
3 larger, enormous, small
4 find, scratch, point
5 cut, wiped out, injured
6 ungloved

What does *it* mean?

Students whose language contains no neuter third person pronoun may have special trouble with the skill practised in this exercise. It would be a good idea to let the students compare their answers in pairs or small groups once they have attempted the exercise individually. Answers:

1 the 'felt' image   5 the doctor's touch
2 a hole   6 the affected side
3 the 'felt' image   7 the fact
4 the 'felt' image   8 the ungloved object

Inference

This is a rather difficult exercise. It is best done in groups so that students can pool their resources. Answers:

1 The 'felt' image becomes clearer when you move (line 14–19); if you get a hole in one of your teeth, this becomes part of the 'felt' image. (line 26–9)
2 The 'felt' image becomes clearer when you move; if you lie still it is difficult to imagine the 'felt' image (lines 10–13). So paralysed people, who do not move, must have very vague 'felt' images.
3 In the example about gloves, the patient uses the hand on the affected side to put the glove on the other hand. So the affected side is not paralysed.
4 The patient feels the doctor's touch (line 63–4)
5 In the example about gloves, the patient is not helped by the fact that he can see his left hand.

ADDITIONAL ACTIVITIES
Learning about your 'felt' image

This is a listening comprehension exercise that will illustrate some of the ideas in the text. It can also provide a basis for group discussion or writing practice.

Read each instruction out to the class and let them follow it. Afterwards, they can do either the *Group discussion* or the *Writing practice* suggested below.

1 Stand up and stand on one foot. Bend the other leg at the knee so the lower part of the leg is parallel with the floor. Count to ten. Now close your eyes and see how long you can remain standing.
2 Sit down. Hold your hands out at arms' length, two feet (60 cm) apart. Bring your index fingers together until they touch. Put your hands two feet apart again. Close your eyes and try to make your index fingers touch again.
3 Take a piece of string or a small strip of paper. Make a circle that you think is the size of your wrist. Measure it against your wrist to see how good your guess was.
4 Without standing up, list the four people sitting closest to you, and

yourself, in order of height. Now stand up and check how accurate your order was.

5 Take a piece of paper and make two circles on it. The circles should represent the distance you think to be between your eyes. Now punch holes in the paper at the place of the circles and try to look through the holes.

Teachers working with younger students, in classes where they do not wish to organize a group discussion, may prefer to use this as a 'warm-up' activity instead.

Group discussion

Divide the class into groups of four or five once they have finished the previous exercise. Each group should pool its findings from that exercise and try to draw some conclusions in a short written report. Some points to consider:

– What points in the text were illustrated by the tasks in the last exercise?
– What did the exercise show you about your own image of your body?

Writing practice

If you do not wish to do the *Group discussion* exercise in class, you may like to follow up the first activity with written homework. Ask each student to report the results of the tasks she did, and to try to draw some conclusions. The students may wish to refer to the vocabulary in the original text to help them.

Part 4   Narrative: What happened

Unit 13   The diamond

You may want to set the scene briefly before the students read the text, by asking them where Johannesburg is, what the natural resources of South Africa are, and where Alexandria is.

Summary skills

Once the students have done this individually, they can compare answers in small groups. This will probably help most of the students who have made mistakes to correct them before you discuss the answers with the entire class.

Answers: 1h, 2a, 3j, 4i, 5d, 6b

Making connections

It might be a good idea to let students compare their answers in small groups after doing this exercise individually. Answers:
1 *His father* means Ephraim's father's father (Ephraim's grandfather).
2 *This* means to cut a diamond perfectly.
3 *Ones* means members of Ephraim's family.
4 *His* means a senior person.
5 *It* means the stone.

Inference

In correcting this exercise, it will help the students if you find out which questions have been answered incorrectly, and let the students tell you why those answers are wrong.
Answers:
1 No. (It says 'brothers', but does not say how many.)
2 Yes. (They were diamond merchants.)
3 Yes. (He worked for his uncle Ben.)
4 No.
5 Yes. (His brothers and sisters married and had families.)

6   Yes. (He lived alone in the family house.)
7   Yes. (Nothing was expected of him.)
8   No. (The text only speaks of one daughter, but does not say whether she was an only child.)
9   Yes. (In Alexandria.)
10   Yes. (He only met her after he had cut the diamond.)

Opinions and feelings

Again, it will help students to learn the skill practised in this exercise if you find out where mistakes have been made and help the students to see why those answers were wrong.
   Answers: 1d, 2f, 3j, 4c, 5g, 6e, 7b

ADDITIONAL ACTIVITIES

What will happen next?

Divide the students into groups of about five. Their task is to write an ending for Ephraim's story. But there is a twist: they must incorporate four of these elements into their ending
– a misunderstanding
– a car accident
– a war
– a stolen handbag
– a baby
(Tell them that they need only write down the bare facts of their ending, so that they can tell it to the rest of the class.)
   If you wish, the class can vote on which group has produced the best ending.

Vocabulary work

There are several words in the text which are used metaphorically, or in ways that are not very familiar to students at this level. Your class will doubtless have understood the meaning of the words, but could not necessarily use them with the meanings they have in the text.
   Suggested procedure: Ask the students to look at the word *brilliant*, line 5, and tell you what it means. Then ask them if they can use the same word with a different meaning. In the first case, they will probably say something like 'intelligent' or 'clever', and in the second case will

come out with sentences like 'It was a day of brilliant sunshine' or 'The colours were brilliant'.

Tell the students that there are several other words in the text like this. Ask them, individually or in pairs or groups, to make at least two new sentences with each of these words (or any others they may find in the text):

– cut out (line 7)
– trade (line 8)
– stone (line 15)
– edge (line 22)
– closed (line 42)
– infected (line 43)

Walk around the room to answer students' questions as they work. They will probably want to ask you things like 'Can you use "edge" in this way with anything besides "voice"?' (No.) 'What word do I use in the sentence "The wound was infected .... several kinds of bacteria?"' (with).

You may want to ask for volunteers to read some of their sentences at the end of the exercise.

Writing practice

Ephraim's story is written very much in the style of a folk tale. Perhaps your students would enjoy writing down folk tales from their own country or countries. They can look back at the text to see what tenses, sentence structures, and connecting devices the author uses.

Unit 14   Dear editors

You might introduce students to the theme of this unit by getting them to vote on this question:

'How many of you think that the best way to discipline children is to spank them when they need it?' 'How many of you think children should never be spanked?'

Summary skills 1

There is no single right answer to this question. Perhaps the best approach is the following: Let each student work on her own to produce a summary sentence. Then ask for a volunteer to read out a sentence. (Accept any sentence that comes close to summarizing the passage: it is the work done to get to the sentence, rather than the sentence itself, that is the most important aspect of this exercise, but students may feel cheated if there is not some check on their work once they have finished.) Then ask if anyone else has a slightly different sentence. Go on doing this until everyone who wants to contribute a different way of phrasing the summary has spoken.

As a reference, here are two summary sentences produced by native English speakers:
1 A two-year-old was cured of scratching by a teacher who rewarded the child's victims and ignored her.
2 Children will stop bullying if you pay attention to their victims.

Summary skills 2

Answers: 1a, 2f, 3b, 4h, 5a, 6g, 7c, 8i, 9d, 10i, 11a, 12f, 13e

Guessing unknown words 1

This is a short introductory exercise to help students see what kinds of reasoning they can use in order to guess unknown words. Answers:
1 scratch
2 understand
3 sad, unhappy, hurt

Guessing unknown words 2

Students get less help in this exercise. Perhaps you would like them to compare answers with one another before checking the exercise with the entire class.

Answers (in these or other words):
1 top
2 pleasure, a feeling of power
3 sweet
4 arms; children, lovers, a boyfriend, a girlfriend, a husband, a wife, mother and father
5 no; tiring, time-consuming, troublesome

Dividing sentences

This is a bit different from the previous *Dividing sentences* exercises, in that students decide whether a division should be made or not. It happens that

in this text the author does not use commas where many people might do so; unless the students can supply the pauses in places where a comma would go, they will have difficulty understanding the sentence. Answers:
1 Division. (The clause beginning 'If...' ends here.)
2 No division. ('and' joins 'fly in terror from her' to 'cower screaming in corners'.)
3 No division. (The part of the sentence after 'and' is elliptical: it means 'her victim would be given a sweet'.)
4 Division. ('cradling her in my arms' is rather like an interruption in the main sentence, where the principal elements are 'I gathered up the little one / and said, "Nice, nice sweetie"/ and I popped it into her mouth.')
5 Division. ('when she got nothing' is like an explanation of 'then'.)
6 No division. ('and' joins 'rewarding' to 'giving more attention to the injured one'.)

Accurate comprehension

This exercise will help students learn to be careful of making unwarranted inferences. The 'doesn't say' option means that they cannot base their answers simply on a vague impression of the text.
   Answers: 1F, 2F, 3T, 4DS, 5DS

ADDITIONAL ACTIVITIES

Class discussion

Divide the class into groups of four or five (a group can have only three people in it, but this is not so satisfactory). In this exercise, five points will be discussed. Each student will have the responsibility for one or more points. She must make sure that all the other members of the group express themselves on that point, and make brief notes on the opinions expressed (she need not note who expressed each opinion).
   Distribute the points for discussion, either by giving each group an envelope you have prepared, with the five points written on separate slips of paper; or by assigning numbers 1 to 5 to the students and then writing the numbered points on the board. Students will probably work better if you give them a realistic time limit for this exercise. You may want each group to report briefly on their discussion at the end of the exercise, or to hand in their notes. Here are the points:
1 In some countries teachers are allowed to punish children physically. In other countries this is against the law. Which is best? Why?
2 What are the things you would look for in choosing a nursery school for a two-and-a-half-year-old?

3 Imagine you are babysitting with a two-year-old. You have taken her
   to play in a sand pit in the park. An older child takes her toys and hits
   her. What do you do?
4 In many countries special arrangements are made for the education of
   handicapped children. In some countries special facilities are also
   provided for very gifted children. Should both these groups of children
   have equal chances of special education?
5 What were the best and worst things about your own schooling when
   you were very small?

Vocabulary work

Ask the students to choose four or five words to learn from the text. For
each word they should:
– look it up in a good dictionary
– think of another word that means approximately the same
– write what they think the differences between the two words are.

Writing practice

Ask the students to write an account of an interesting (good or bad)
experience they have had with a child, or of an interesting experience
they had when they were children themselves.

Unit 15   Great operatic disasters

You may wish to introduce the theme of the unit by asking the class to
define for you what an opera is, and perhaps give you the names of a
few famous operas.

Summary skills 1

Once the students have done this exercise individually, it would be good to
let them compare answers among themselves before checking the answers
with the entire class. Answers (in these or other words):

1 soprano, main singer   5 trampoline
2 stage, theatre   6 bounced, came
3 mattress   7 leave
4 jumped, threw herself

Summary skills 2

This would be a good exercise for the students to do in groups. Answers: c, e, i, b, f, d, a, h. (g does not belong to the San Francisco story.) Make sure they realize that they must turn the page to find some of the pictures.

Guessing unknown words

You might have the students compare answers in pairs or small groups before correcting the exercise with the whole class.
Answers: 1m, 2f, 3l, 4i, 5b, 6j, 7k, 8d

Accurate comprehension

Some of the questions in this exercise help the students make inferences from what is clearly stated in the text; others make them read details in the text more carefully. When correcting, you will help the students if you discuss the 'why' of each answer.
Answers: 1T, 2T, 3F ('It is said...'), 4F ('...is *thought* to be...'), 5T, 6F (if they had liked opera, they would certainly have known or learnt something about the story), 7F (it was the fault of the producer).

ADDITIONAL ACTIVITIES

Personal disasters

Divide the class into groups of four to six students. Tell the students they will have a few minutes to think of a story of some embarrassing experience. The experience can be the student's own or someone else's, and it does not have to be true. Each student should tell the story to her group; the group will vote on the funniest story, which will then be told to the whole class.

Vocabulary work

Ask the students to choose four or five words to learn from the text. They should tell another student the reasons for their choices, and write two sentences with each word.

Writing practice

Ask the students to write down the stories they have told in the *Personal disasters* exercise.

Unit 16   The poisoning of Michigan

This is perhaps the most difficult text in the book. However, doing the exercises should help the students to understand the text better, and give them ways of approaching difficult texts that they encounter outside the classroom.

As a 'warm-up', you might want to list the following things on the board:
— tap water
— bread
— frozen peas
— sweets
— fruit juice labelled '100% juice'
and ask the students which of these things are likely to contain added chemicals. (Answer: all of them. Tap water often contains chlorine used to purify it, bread often contains preservatives, frozen peas and sweets often contain colouring agents, and fruit juice is often bought wholesale in concentrated form and then packaged after the addition of chlorinated water.)

Summary skills 1

You may wish to have the students do this exercise in small groups so as to pool their resources. Answers (in these or different words):
2   MgO and PBB stored in the same warehouse
5   PBB mixed with cattle feed
7   Cattle ate poisoned feed
9   Milk and beef from diseased cattle sold to public
11   One farmer discovered why his animals sickened and died
13   A thorough investigation showed that PBB did damage human health

Summary skills 2

Now that students have reviewed the chronological sequence of events in the story, this exercise will help them to focus on the chain of causes. Again, you may wish them to work in groups.

Answers: People did their jobs badly at points 2, 3, 4, 5, 12.

Guessing unknown words

When you are correcting this exercise, find out what mistakes were made

and discuss why they were made. This will help students the next time they need to guess unknown words.
Answers: 1k, 2a, 3i, 4l, 5e, 6h, 7c, 8m

Why?

This exercise will require students to make inferences about the facts actually contained in the text. Answers:
1 –The trade name of PBB (Firemaster), written on the bags, was similar to the trade name of MgO (Nutrimaster).
  –Some of the lettering on the bags was smudged.
  –Some of the mixer operators could not read very well.
  –PBB and MgO are similar in appearance.
  –The sacks the PBB was packed in were almost identical to the sacks MgO was packed in.
2 Each farmer whose cattle were ill assumed that his were the only ones to suffer, and did not communicate with other farmers about it.
3 Most farmers have no specialized knowledge about chemicals. Only one farmer in Michigan with 'exceptional knowledge of chemicals' was able to discover the reason why his cattle died.
4 The sort of damage PBB does builds up gradually over a long time. Most doctors were not used to this sort of disease, so they did not recognize it.

Negative expressions

Recognizing negative expressions is a 'mini-skill' that can improve students' comprehension greatly. You may want to use this exercise as a diagnostic test, and write other, similar exercises for those students who have difficulty with this one. Answers:
1 *what they believed*; It was not magnesium oxide.
2 *should have been*; The chemicals were not kept in separate warehouses.
3 *Neither...nor*; Shorty did not notice the difference, and the men who handled the bags did not notice the difference.
4 *failed*; They did not understand a chronic toxicosis.

ADDITIONAL ACTIVITIES

Compensation and prevention

Divide the class into groups of five or so. Give them two minutes for each group to elect a chairperson (who must see that the tasks are done and that everyone in the group is consulted) and a secretary (who must note down the results of the discussion). Then give the groups these tasks to perform:

1 Here is a list of people or organizations who made mistakes leading to the 'poisoning of Michigan'. Decide what each did (or did not do) to be considered guilty in this affair.
   – The Michigan Chemical Corporation.
   – The company that made the cattle feed.
   – The State of Michigan.
   – Farmers who sent diseased animals to market.
   – Doctors who told PBB victims there was nothing wrong with them.
2 One billion dollars ($1,000,000,000) has been awarded to PBB victims by the courts. Your task is to decide what percentage of this money should be paid by each person or group in Question 1.
3 Make at least four recommendations to the legislature of the State of Michigan for new laws to ensure that this sort of situation cannot happen again.

Make sure that everyone understands the tasks before they begin. Then walk around the room to answer questions while the students are working. Try not to intrude on a group unless your help is requested, and do not correct the students' English mistakes at this time. You can do more controlled work on grammar, etc., at another time; here the students should be developing their fluency and their ability to make themselves understood in English.

The students will probably enjoy sharing the results of their work with the other groups when the exercise is finished.

Vocabulary work

You may wish students to do one or both of these exercises.

1 Below are four connecting words or phrases from the article. Write sentences as instructed.
   a) *In fact* (line 19): Write two sentences and use this phrase in the second one.
   b) *Given that* (line 47): Write a sentence using this phrase.
   c) *Yet* (line 56): Write two sentences, beginning the second one with *Yet;* or write one sentence with *yet* in the middle, after a comma or a semicolon.
   d) *Consequently* (line 81): Write two sentences, beginning the second one with *Consequently;* or write one sentence with *consequently* in the middle, after a semicolon.
2 Choose five words to learn from the article. Look up each word in a dictionary, write down in what sort of document you might write it yourself, and write a sentence using it.

Writing practice

Encourage students to refer back to text for help with grammar as they do
one of these exercises:

1 Write about a disaster that has happened in your own country or a place
   you know.
2 Imagine a disaster in your own country or a place you know and write
   about it.
3 Write part of a science fiction story including a disaster.

Part 5 Persuasion: Why you should do it

Unit 17 The challenge

You may want to introduce the theme of the unit by asking students to tell you what they would look for in a new car. Write the qualities on the board as they give them. Then have the class vote on which is the most important.

Summary skills

Doing this exercise will help students to organize for themselves the mass of details in the text. Answers:

	Audi 80 GLS	BL Princess
Price		✓
Reliability	✓	
Comfort:		
elbow room	✓	
headroom	✓	
legroom (rear)		✓
Speed:		
0–60 mph	✓	
50–70 mph in 3rd gear	✓	
Economy:		
type of petrol used	✓	
mpg	✓	
money saved over 30,000 miles	✓	

Guessing unknown words

Some of these questions guide students through a reasoning process to help them guess the meaning of a word. In the questions that do not (numbers 3, 4, 5, 6 and 7), it is not a good idea to ask the students to tell you how they arrived at their correct conclusions. First of all, there may be different paths to the same end; and secondly, articulating the process may be too difficult a task for most students. Answers (in these or other words):

1   came upon by accident
2   what its virtues are, how good it is
3   disappointed, unhappy
4   not as good, less good
5   lazy, irresponsible, idle
6   car
7   direct, simple, uncomplicated
8   drive it, test it, put it to a test

Inference

This exercise may be a little difficult for some students. It is probably best to let the class do it in pairs or threes.
   Answers: 1f, 2c, 3g, 4a, 5d

ADDITIONAL ACTIVITIES

Class survey

In this exercise, each student must do a survey of the rest of the class, walking around and asking everyone else a question. When the survey is finished, each student reports to the class. Here are 15 questions; if there are more than 15 people in your class, you can give the same question to more than one person and tell them to compare their answers before giving a joint report.

1   Do you drive? Do you / would you enjoy driving?
2   Would you / do you enjoy having a chauffeur? Why?
3   Would you rather have a fast, not very pretty car, or a beautiful, not very fast car? Why?
4   Do you think there will be more or fewer cars on the road by the year 2020? Why?
5   Would you buy a small solar-powered car for local driving if it was available? Why?
6   Do you wear a safety belt in the car: always / usually / sometimes / never? Why?

7   In some countries it is illegal for a child under ten years of age to sit in the front seat of a moving car. Do you think this is good? Why?

8   Should the law require that children always wear seat belts when a car is moving? Why?

9   What is your favourite colour for a car? What do you think this says about your personality?

10   What is the speed limit on motorways in your country? Do most people observe the limit?

11   Have you ever bought a used car? Would you do it (again)? Why?

12   Do you enjoy watching car races? Can you say why?

13   If you had the money to buy and maintain any car you wanted, what car would you buy? Why?

14   Have you ever driven in a foreign country? If so, was it difficult for you to adjust to the differences?

15   In some countries, you must take driving lessons at an approved driving school before taking a test and getting a licence. Do you think this is good? Why?

Car design

Divide the students into small groups and have them design the ideal car for a traffic jam. It can be as outlandish as they wish. When they have finished, they must try to 'sell' their car to the rest of the class.

Vocabulary work

You may wish your students to do one or both of these exercises:

1   Read lines 4–10 of the advertisement again and notice how the words *Naturally* (line 6) and *however* (line 8) are used to construct the argument of the text. Look these two words up in a good dictionary. Think of translations in your own language if this helps you. Then write two short paragraphs using these words in the same way as they are used in the advertisement.

2   Choose four or five words from the text to learn. Look them up in a good dictionary. Write at least one sentence with each word; if the word can be used in more than one way (for instance, as a verb and a noun), write more than one sentence.

Writing practice

This exercise will give students some practice in writing a comparative report which tries to persuade the reader to a particular viewpoint. Ask them to imagine that a friend has asked for help in making a choice between two

things they are familiar with. For example:
– vacation spots
– schools
– jobs
– bicycles
– stereos
– pocket calculators
The student should write a letter of advice to her friend, comparing the two
things, and organizing the comments under headings like those in the
advertisement (Reliability, Comfort, etc.). At the end of the letter, she
should give definite advice in favour of one or the other choice.

Unit 18   Go ahead–read this

You might set the scene for this text by asking students what the advantages
and drawbacks of living in a big city are. Pollution is bound to come up as
one of the drawbacks.

Reading for specific information

Give the students a minute or so to look at the table without marking
anything on it or reading the text. Then tell them to fill in the table as
quickly as they can by finding the answers in the text. You may wish them
to compare answers with one another before checking with you. Answers
(in these or other words):

Problem	Exact cause	Result	If there were no private cars, ...
Air pollution	Carbon monoxide & benzpyrene & nitrates	Poor health (cancer)	Much less pollution
Space pollution	Garages & highways = 30% of downtown Boston	Crowding?	More homes, gardens, places to work and play
Noise pollution	Horns, engines, traffic noise	People are losing hearing faster	Old people would hear better
Accidents	Text does not say	Deaths	Fewer deaths

Guessing unknown words

This is a slightly more complicated exercise than some of the other *Guessing unknown words* tasks. You may wish the students to do the exercise in pairs or small groups of three to four.
    Answers: 1e, 2d, 3i, 4c, 5g, 6b, 7j, 8f

Accurate comprehension

This exercise obliges students to take a careful look at some parts of the text that can cause understanding problems if they are read carelessly.
    Answers: 1F, 2T, 3T, 4F, 5T

ADDITIONAL ACTIVITIES

Brainstorming

This activity is best done in groups of about five people. Suggested procedure:
1   Ask the students if they think that distributing leaflets to passengers already using public transportation is the best way to get something done about pollution. When they agree that it isn't, tell them that they will have the task of finding better ways.
2   Divide the class into groups of about five. Ask each group to spend two minutes electing a secretary who will write things down. They then have ten or 15 minutes to think of as many ways as possible to bring the anti-pollution message to a wider public, and to state the message effectively. Any idea, no matter how nonsensical it seems, should be expressed: it is quantity, not quality, that matters at this stage. A seemingly ridiculous idea can sometimes provoke a creative and practical one.
3   When the time limit you have set is reached, ask the groups to choose the five best ideas from their stock. Each of the groups then reports its ideas to the rest of the class.

Writing practice

Ask students to write an imaginary letter to their city councillor about one of the following things:
1   Ask that more bicycle lanes be reserved in the streets of the city centre.
2   Protest against a planned major road that is to replace your quiet little street.

3 Proposals have been made for a reduction of bus services in your city. This will mean fewer buses per hour. Protest.
4 There are not enough protected pedestrian crossings in your city centre. Ask for more.

Unit 19   Save the children

To introduce the theme of this unit, you might ask if someone in the class knows what a charity is, or tell the class if no one knows. Ask them if they know the names of any charities and what they do.

Summary skills

This exercise gives the students the opportunity to choose for themselves which aspect of text they wish to focus on. Have the students do the exercise individually first; then ask each student to find at least one other person who has chosen the same topic as she has. Answers will vary somewhat, but the students' final notes should look something like this:

1 SCHOOL
  – it is miles away
  – Maria cannot go because she's needed at home
  – sponsorship will buy school supplies
  – a combined sponsorship can build a school

2 MARIA'S MOTHER
  – has lost her husband and two children because the family could not afford a doctor
  – needs Maria's help at home
  – could farm her land if given tools and guidance
  – could earn money if given help

3 FOOD AND WATER
  – not enough food for Maria's family
  – the water available to Maria's family is contaminated
  – food could be grown on Maria's mother's land if tools and guidance were given
  – clean water could be brought to Maria's family if enough sponsorship were received

4   SPONSORING A CHILD
   – costs only 52 pennies a day
   – could help Maria's mother farm her land and earn money
   – combined with other sponsors' money, yours can help people help
     themselves through schools, health facilities, clean water
   – rewards through correspondence, photos, progress reports, know-
     ledge that you're really helping

5   MARIA'S FAMILY LIFE
   – her father, a brother and a sister have died
   – she takes care of her baby brother
   – she helps her mother with the chores

Guessing unknown words

In correcting this exercise, find out what mistakes students have made
and help them see why their answers are wrong. This will help them do
better the next time. Answers: 1c, 2f, 3d, 4j, 5l, 6a, 7g, 8i

Find the reasons... find the ways

This exercise gives the students practice in inference. You may wish to
have them do it in small groups. Answers:
1 – contaminated water
   – not enough food
   – fatigue from too much heavy work
2 Maria's father died because the family could not afford a doctor.
3 – tools for her mother
   – guidance for her mother
   – a school in the village
4 – clean water
   – a health facility
5 – photographs
   – progress reports
   – letters

ADDITIONAL ACTIVITIES

Planning help

This is a group exercise in which the students imagine they are in charge
of planning help for Maria's village.

SUGGESTED PROCEDURE

Divide the students into groups of five or so and give them the following task description. Make sure that they all understand what they have to do. While they are working, move around the classroom to give any help they may need. Do not correct any mistakes they may make in their English; this exercise is for developing fluency, and they can work on the correctness of their English at another time. When the groups have finished (you may want to impose a time limit before they start), ask each group to state and briefly explain their results.

Task: You are the committee in charge of planning aid to Maria's village. Sponsors have been found for all the children; this means that you can help the individual children, but also that you can begin work on larger projects. The problem is that your money from the sponsors does not arrive all at once, but month by month. Here is a list of projects you wish to carry out, and the number of months of money each project will take. You must decide the order in which the projects will be done. Be prepared to tell the rest of the class why you have decided on this order.

1 Tools and seeds for farming – one month
2 Sewing machines so the women can earn money – three months
3 Clean water facilities – six months
4 School building – five months (the government will provide a teacher)
5 Health facility – ten months
6 A radio antenna so the village can get educational programmes and news – two months
7 More land so the village can sell produce in the nearby town – nine months
8 A tractor to help work the new land – five months

Vocabulary work

Ask the students to choose four words or expressions from the advertisement, to look them up in a good dictionary, and to write two sentences using each word.

Writing practice

Have each student write a letter of appeal like the one here, on behalf of her favourite charity. The charity can be real or imaginary.

Unit 20   Two letters

Note that in America most people have to pay their doctors for care given; often people belong to private insurance schemes which reimburse part of their medical expenses.

You may want to get students thinking about the theme of the unit like this: Tell them to imagine that they do not have enough money to pay all their debts. They must make a choice between paying
a) their monthly instalment on the car,
b) their doctor's bill, or
c) their life insurance.
Get the students to vote with a show of hands on which bill they would pay.

Have you got the main ideas?

This exercise covers the main points in the two letters.
    Answers: 1F, 2T, 3F, 4T, 5F

Guessing unknown words

This exercise is a bit more difficult than some of the other *Guessing unknown words;* you may wish for the students to do the exercise in pairs or groups in order to pool their resources. Answers:

1 account	4 ample
2 extend the courtesy	5 alternative
3 ignore	6 collection agency

Inference

Once more, you may wish the students to do this exercise in pairs; the 'cultural' content of the letters may be very new to some students. Answers:
1   Ms Marques is the 'Office Manager'; this would imply that there are other people working in the office.
2   In the first letter, Ms Marques invites the man to make 'partial payments...even small payments'.
3   Ms Marques leaves the man several options in both letters: 'even small payments'; 'send payment, call, or write'. In her last paragraph she does not threaten to turn the account over to a collection agency if he does not pay; but to do so if she has not heard from him.
4   If the account is turned over to a collection agency, the fact will be 'on

[the man's] credit record'. This implies some centralization of credit information.

ADDITIONAL ACTIVITIES

Role play

This exercise takes a little preparation. You will have to copy the role descriptions below: Description A for half of the students, and Descriptions 1B, 2B, and 3B in roughly equal numbers for the other half. The students will work in pairs (A + 1B, A + 2B, A + 3B); but if there is an uneven number in the class, you can give out an extra 1B role and let two students play spouses going to the office together.

Hand out the roles, giving the same role to students seated in the same part of the classroom. Tell them to read the role description and discuss it with one another; answer any questions they have about meaning. Then pair the students up, an A and a B in each pair. Remind them before they begin their conversations that some of them will be standing when the conversation begins and some of them sitting. They can consult their own role description during the conversation but should *not* look at the other person's.

Walk round the classroom while they are doing the exercise, to give help to those who need it. It is not a good idea to interrupt the students during this exercise to correct their English mistakes; let them practise speaking freely with the English they can command.

Students who finish early can form new pairs.

Role descriptions

A   You work in Dr Brown's office. If patients come in to talk about a bill, you ask them to sit down, and you consult their file. You are very understanding if the people seem to be in financial difficulty. However, you must try to get them to begin paying something immediately, if only $1 a week. Experience has proved that the sooner people begin paying, the more likely they are to pay the entire debt. Once the patients agree on payment arrangements, ask them to try not to miss a payment.
Here are some extracts from your files:
Mr/Ms Edmundson owes $200
Mr and Mrs Honeywell owe $350
Mr and Mrs Thompson owe $300
Ms Wells owes $50
Mr/Ms Wood owes $150

1B   You are Mr or Mrs Honeywell. You owe Dr Brown $350 for
     Mrs Honeywell's treatment. Mr Honeywell has been on strike for a
     month. Mrs Honeywell doesn't work, and has two children under
     five at home. Mr Honeywell has been trying to find temporary work
     but has not been successful. You do not want your debt to be
     referred to a collection agency. You can begin paying $50 a month
     when the strike is over. Begin the conversation by saying, 'Hello. I'm
     Mrs (Mr) Honeywell. I'd like to talk to you about my bill.'

2B   You are Mr or Ms Edmundson. You owe Dr Brown $200. You are a
     single parent with a child of six. The child's school fees have just gone
     up; on top of that, your car has broken down and you have
     had to buy another one. You cannot possibly pay the $200 now;
     you would like to pay $20 now and $20 a month until the summer
     (in three months' time). Then you may be able to pay a bit more.
     Begin the conversation by saying, 'Good morning (afternoon). I'm
     Mr (Ms) Edmundson. It's about my bill.'

3B   You are Ms or Mr Wood. You owe Dr Brown $150. You are a
     university student, and have very little money. You cannot borrow
     money from your parents because you have quarrelled with them.
     Your part-time job just gives you enough money to live on, and you
     do not want to take on any more paid work now as your studies
     may suffer. You would like to wait until the summer (three months
     from now), when you will have a full-time job. You can then pay
     off the $150 within two months' time. If the people in the doctor's
     office are really insistent, you may be able to pay $10 a month until
     the summer.

Writing practice

1 Have the students imagine they are the patient or her husband and write
   a reply to the 17 November letter, apologizing for not writing sooner
   and proposing some arrangement for payment.
2 Have the students write another letter from Ms Marques to the patient's
   husband, dated 30 November. He has not answered any of the letters
   and his account is to be turned over to a collection agency.

Part 6   Categories: How things are classified

Unit 21   Elephants

To introduce the subject of the unit, you might give the students 60 seconds to tell you as many things as they can about elephants.

Summary skills 1

It is not really necessary to 'correct' this exercise. But you may want to walk around while the students are working and make sure they are writing down only points that have to do with the subject they have chosen.

Summary skills 2

This exercise will help the students to organize the information found in the text in a more accessible way. Answers:

1a larger	2a smaller
1b flatter forehead	2b rounder forehead
1c bigger ears	2c smaller ears
1d both sexes have tusks; bigger tusks	2d only males have tusks; smaller tusks
1e two projections on trunk	2e one projection on trunk

Guessing unknown words

Remember to find out what the incorrect answers were and help students to see why they were incorrect.
    Answers: 1f, 2c, 3j, 4k, 5o, 6b, 7e, 8h

Accurate comprehension

This exercise will help students to read detail carefully and to avoid making unwarranted inferences.
    Answers: 1T, 2F, 3DS, 4T, 5DS, 6T

ADDITIONAL ACTIVITIES

Describing and guessing

If there are more than about 12 students, you will probably want to divide the class into groups of around six to ten for this exercise.

Give the students five minutes. During this time each student thinks of an animal and how she can describe it. Then each student stands up in turn and describes the animal without giving its name. This description should be about one to two minutes long. The others must write down what animal they think it is. After everyone has spoken, the group can check how many right answers there were.

Designing an animal

In groups of about five, the students design the perfect animal for one of these uses:
– a pet who lives in a flat in the city
– an animal to take mountain climbing
– a pet for a very organized person
– a pet that costs no money to keep
When they have finished, they describe their animal (with drawings if they wish) to the rest of the class.

Vocabulary work

Ask the students to find about five words to learn from the text. These should be words that could be used in an article that was *not* about elephants. Have them look the words up in a dictionary and write a sentence using each one.

Writing practice

Have the students write a short article comparing two things or people that they know well. The article should describe the similarities and differences between the two.

Unit 22　Airports

To introduce the article, you might tell the students that they are going to read about airports, and ask them to think of some of the words that might come up.

Summary skills 1

You may wish students to compare answers with one another before checking the table with the whole class.

	Gatwick	*Heathrow*	*Stansted*
Capacity	16m passengers a year	30m passengers a year	not given
Passengers in May	687,700	2.2 million +	not given
% rise in passengers since May last year	26%	7%	13.9%
Passengers this year to the end of May	6.8 million	not given	not given

Summary skills 2

Answers:
1　whole-charter flights
2　Heathrow

Guessing unknown words

You may wish students to work in pairs or small groups for this exercise.
Answers:
1　marked
2　boosted
3　scheduled
4　issue
5　reciprocal

Making connections

This exercise should help students in two ways:
- It will give them some practice in the skill of recognizing what words like *she* and *this* refer to.
- It will alert them to the fact that this is an area where they may be making mistakes in their reading, and help them to be more careful here in the future.

Answers:
1 Heathrow's
2 May
3 Stansted's rate of growth in May (= *It*); the rate of growth in May (= *that*)
4 the move of all whole-charter flights
5 the expansion programme
6 Gatwick
7 boosting the number of scheduled flights to and from Gatwick

Accurate comprehension

This exercise will help students to read detail carefully and to avoid making unwarranted inferences.
Answers: 1T, 2F, 3T, 4T, 5DS

ADDITIONAL ACTIVITIES

Class survey

In this exercise, each student must do a survey of the rest of the class, walking around and asking everyone else a question. When the survey is finished, each student reports to the class. Here are 15 questions; if there are more than 15 people in your class, you can give the same question to more than one person and tell them to compare their answers before giving a joint report.
1 Have you flown in an aeroplane? If so, how old were you when you flew for the first time?
2 Have you ever taken a charter flight? Would you take one (again)? Why?
3 Would you like to fly in Concorde? Why?
4 Would you enjoy being an airline pilot for a year? Why?
5 What would you rather do – pilot a plane or pilot a glider (= like a plane but with no engine)?
6 Do you think an airline hostess's job is exciting? Why?

7   Would you rather travel by train or by plane? Why?
8   Do you / would you feel safer in a plane or in a car on a fast road?
    Why?
9   What are the advantages of air travel?
10 What are the disadvantages of air travel?
11 Can you name a famous male aeroplane pilot? a famous female
    aeroplane pilot?
12 Would you feel as comfortable flying with a male aeroplane pilot as
    a female one?
13 Would you rather have a hostess (woman) or a steward (man) serving
    you in a plane, or doesn't it matter?
14 If you could have a free aeroplane ticket to anywhere in the world,
    where would you go?
15 If it became possible in your lifetime for you to take a rocket to the
    moon, would you like to do it? Why?

Vocabulary work

Ask students to find three new words, or three words they know used in
new ways, in the text. They should look these words up in a dictionary
and write a sentence using each word. The sentences should not concern
airports or planes.

Unit 23   The trials of an O in a world of Xs

To introduce this text, you might have the students read the first paragraph
of the introduction, and then ask for a few volunteers to describe a situation
where they have felt different from everyone else.

Make sure the students understand the meaning of 'X' and 'O' as
explained in the second paragraph.

Summary skills

You may wish students to do this exercise in groups, so they can pool
their resources.

Answers: 1f, 2h, 3d, 4a, 5i, 6g, 7e, 8c, 9b

Guessing unknown words

The correction of this exercise can be a learning activity if you find out what wrong answers were chosen and help the students to see why they were wrong.
 Answers: 1a, 2f, 3c, 4d, 5g

General to particular

This exercise is a bit difficult. Doing it in pairs might make the students feel more confident.
 Answers: a3, b5, c7, d1, e3

ADDITIONAL ACTIVITIES

Sketches

1 Divide the class into groups of four or five. Each group is going to devise a sketch in which one of them is an 'O' and the others are all 'Xs'. They should begin by taking ten minutes to decide
 – in what way the O is different from the Xs.
 – what sort of work, school, team or organization they are in.
 – exactly what situation they are going to represent.
 – who is going to be the O and who the Xs.
 Each X should then decide on her attitude towards the 'O': tolerant, hostile, sceptical, friendly... .
2 The students then have only five minutes in which to prepare their actual sketch. This time limit will keep them from presenting something they have written, and will keep the language spontaneous.
3 Each group presents their sketch for the rest of the class, first as a mime with no words. When they have done this the class has a few minutes to say what they think was going on.
4 Then they give the sketch again, this time with words.

Vocabulary work

Ask each student to choose four or five words to learn from the text. She should tell another student in what other context the words might be used. The students should each look their words up in a dictionary, and write a sentence or two with each word.

Writing practice

Ask the students to do one of these exercises:
1 Write about a situation where you were an O in a world of Xs. Describe what happened, but also say what it was the Xs misunderstood about you, and in what ways your reactions were different from theirs.
2 Write an imaginary story of an O and some Xs. These can be categories of people who really exist, or you can invent a new sort of person, as in a science fiction story.

Unit 24   Wonder wander

To introduce this unit, you might give the students three minutes to tell you as many things as they can that can be found on the streets of a town.

Summary skills 1

This will help the students define the broad divisions in the poem.
Answers: 1, 9, 14, 19, 24

Summary skills 2

This will make the students reread the poem more carefully. Answers:

	children	business men	young girls	young men	me
thinking of future			✓	✓	
thinking of present	✓	.			✓
walking without definite direction	✓		✓		✓
walking without stopping		✓		✓	
have a plan		✓		✓	
have no plan	✓		✓		✓

	children	business men	young girls	young men	me
looking at things	✓		✓	✓	✓
not looking at things		✓			

Guessing unknown words

You may wish to ask students to compare answers before correcting this exercise with the whole class.
Answers:
1 leather; documents / letters / papers
2 stop
3 bird / fowl ('chicken' is also a plausible answer given what the students know)
4 bird

Families of words

This is a suitable exercise for group work. Answers:
1 stroll, shoes, stride, parade, wander, soft-shoed, easy-legged, sidewalk
2 talk, voices, whisper
3 ducks, geese, bird-trees, puppy dogs, lady bugs, turkey hens, sea-gull
4 clothes, hats, dresses, (shoes), pockets, (soft-shoed)
5 eyeing, wild eyed, glances, watching, see

Attitudes and feelings 1

This exercise is designed to stimulate discussion in the classroom. There are really no 'right' answers. The answer to the first question might be 'business men' or 'young men'; the answer to the second question might be 'children' or 'herself'. You can handle the exercise in several ways; here are two examples:
1 Get a show-of-hands vote on the first question. Have each student find another student who has given the same answer, and discuss the reasons for two minutes; then have all the students change partners. This time they might be with someone who has a different point of view. They get two more minutes to exchange views and return to their seats. Handle the second question in the same way.
2 An open-class discussion. One way to make sure students listen to one

another is to have them observe the following rule: no one can give her own opinion until she has restated the opinion of the last person to speak, to the satisfaction of that person.

Attitudes and feelings 2

This is an exercise that can profitably be done in a group; it will probably engender a certain amount of discussion. Answers:

children (e)	young men (f)
business men (h)	me (b)
young girls (a)	

ADDITIONAL ACTIVITIES

Vocabulary work

Ask students to choose four or five words to learn from the text. They should look the words up in a good dictionary and find out, from the dictionary or elsewhere, if the words could be used
– in a business letter.
– in a conversation with a six-year old.
They should try to use the words in the next exercise if they are appropriate; or write a sentence or two using each word if not.

Writing practice

This poem is about people walking in a town. Ask the students to write a poem or story about walking in a different place, e.g. the forest, the mountains, the country, a big city. They can describe different people walking in different ways if they wish.